61 Rabbits

Paula Jeffery

Copyright © 2017 Paula Jeffery
All rights reserved.

ISBN-13: 978-1973940081
ISBN-10: 1973940086

Dedicated to
Ava Rose Jeffery
my favourite bunny
(card 25)

61 Rabbits was conceived and born via the ICAD challenge. But what on earth is ICAD?

The Daisy Yellow Index-Card-a-Day Challenge takes place, online and annually during June and July and the idea is to do something creative on a common or garden index card for 61 days. It was founded by Tammy Garcia of Daisy Yellow Art (daisyyellowart.com) in 2011 as, in her own words,

"…a way to inspire people to add creative work INTO the daily flow of life, to make it so darned normal that you keep going all year. There is a camaraderie and a collective energy, so positive, in knowing that you are doing art and other people around the globe are working on the same challenge.

Challengers tell me that playing on a simple index card each day, building that daily creative rhythm, is energizing and life altering. It will positively impact the way that you approach your daily creative practice."

Tammy suggests "that if you aren't doing creative work on a regular basis, you can use the challenge to kick-start a daily practice. If your once-beloved art time has disintegrated, you can use the challenge to get back into the groove. Already a wickedly busy artist? Leverage the energy of the challenge to refresh + pump up the volume on the art you are already doing!!! Use ICAD to experiment in a new medium, make flash cards to learn a language, draw cartoons about kangaroos, explore a theme, write 61 pieces of found poetry or play with mixed media collage. The options are literally never-ending."

During my own artistic journey there have been two or three significant turning points, the earliest one was discovering ICAD. It was 2014 and I was in my late fifties. I'd never been any 'good' at art and would have been one of those people who proclaimed that they 'couldn't draw a straight line'. Although I took art at school the art teacher considered me so useless that I wasn't allowed to take my art exam which coloured my attitude to any art endeavours as an adult. Art just wasn't my thing. However, I did have a love of crafts and was always messing about making something from needlework and knitting to wood and metalwork.

So it was while I was trawling YouTube watching craft videos that I came across art journalling. Now although it had the word art in the title it looked like something I could do, a visual diary and you didn't need to be an artist. It was all about collages, words and splashes of paint. I thought it was something that even I, as a non-artist, could manage. I joined a group of art journallers online and it was there that a member posted up a photo of one of her journal pages. She'd stuck in one of her ICADS and worked around that. I had no idea what an ICAD was, I thought maybe it was some special kind of card that you bought. I seemed to be the only one that didn't know so I set about researching and discovered the Daisy Yellow website and Facebook group and learned about Tammy's challenge.

That first summer joining ICAD was such an eye-opener. Life changing is such a cliche these days but I truly believe it was for me. I joined a huge group of people, mostly women. Some were highly skilled artists, most were not. Everyone was supportive, encouraging and so kind. In ICAD there was no mockery or put downs, it was all support. At first I made and posted 'safe' art, no drawing or painting but collages made from magazines and odd bits of paper. Tammy provides daily prompts which ICADians can feel free to ignore but it can help to concentrate the mind. I tried to follow the prompts and one day wanted to draw an eye, but how? I went to YouTube and typed in 'how to draw an eye' - I watched the tutorials and suddenly realised..oh wow, there is a process here that I can follow, it's not some mysterious force that appears out of the ether, you can really learn this stuff. After the eye I did an elephant and OMG it wasn't really so hard. My art blossomed during those two months and thanks to the wonderful support of my fellow artists I gained more confidence and started drawing graphite portraits.

Three years later and I've travelled down all sorts of artistic roads and although, every year around May, I say I'm too busy to do ICAD this year I always end up getting out my index cards. For me it's freeing, a time to be loose and silly, to just mess about and have fun.

This year, to give myself an extra challenge I decided that I would follow every prompt and in addition stick to a theme of rabbits. What was I thinking? The difficulty has been only equalled by the fun! I've woken up in the middle of the night trying to think of how a rabbit can fit in with the prompt Intersection and then laughed and groaned in unison when my husband came up with the idea of using two rabbit versions of Princess Leia for the prompt Layers! During the 61 days there have been many character developments including gender fluidity and on day 53 our bunny got himself a name, Jasper, as voted for by my fellow ICADians.

Jasper has taken on a life of his own and several people suggested that I publish his cards in a book, so here they are, numbered and each with Tammy's prompt.

With grateful thanks to everyone at ICAD for the most wonderful supportive group who produce the most incredible art and especially to Tammy who puts so much hard work into the organisation of this little jewel nestling in the folds of the internet. Thank you for this gift.

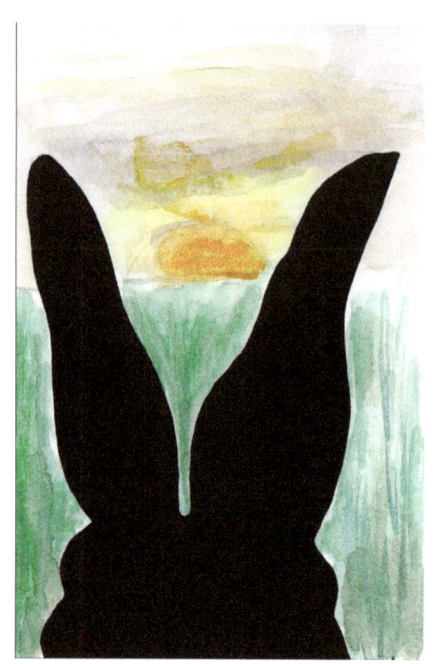

1: Sunset

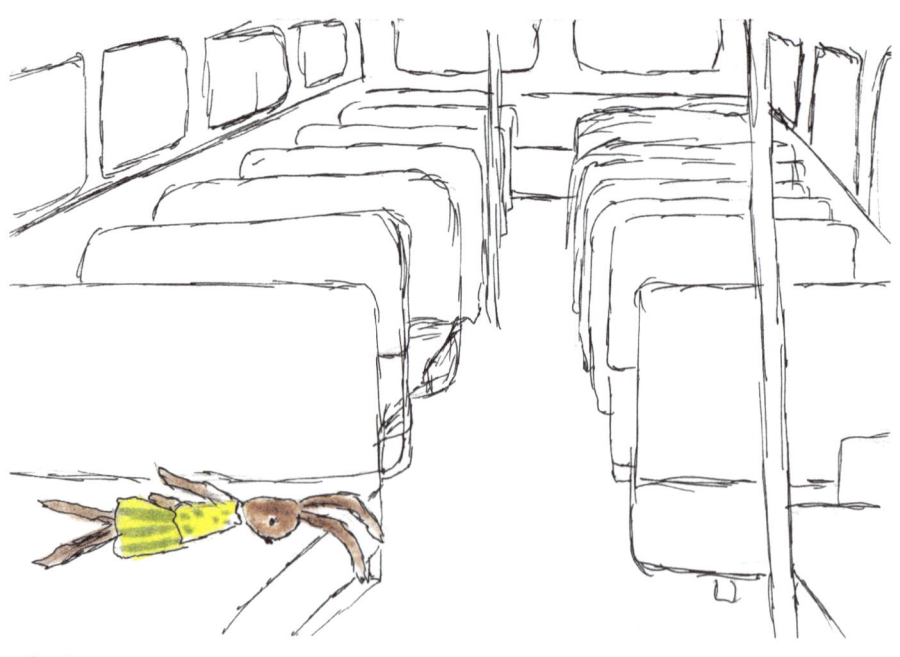

2: Lost

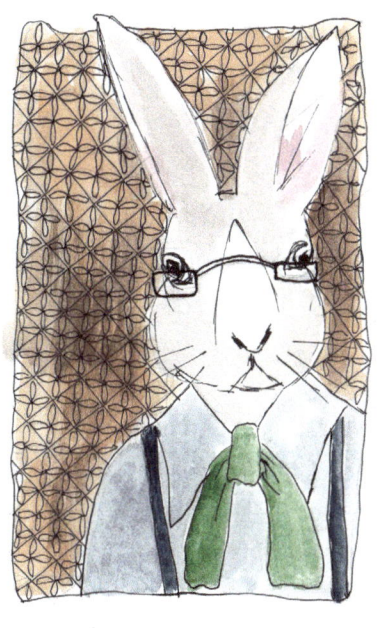

3: Vintage

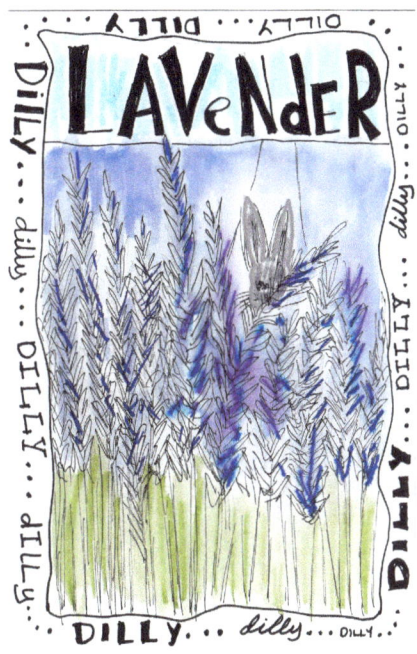

4: Lavender

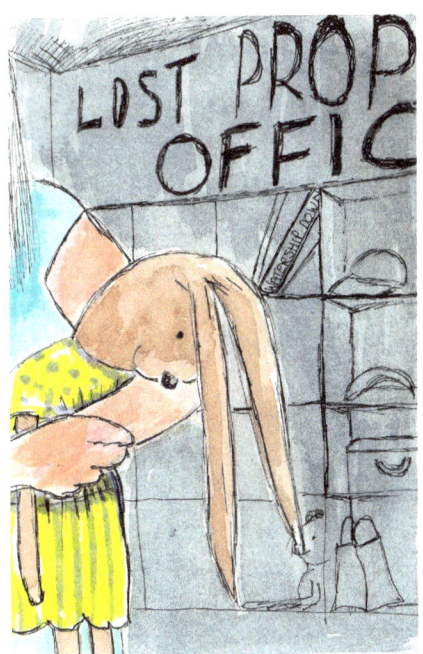

5: Cute

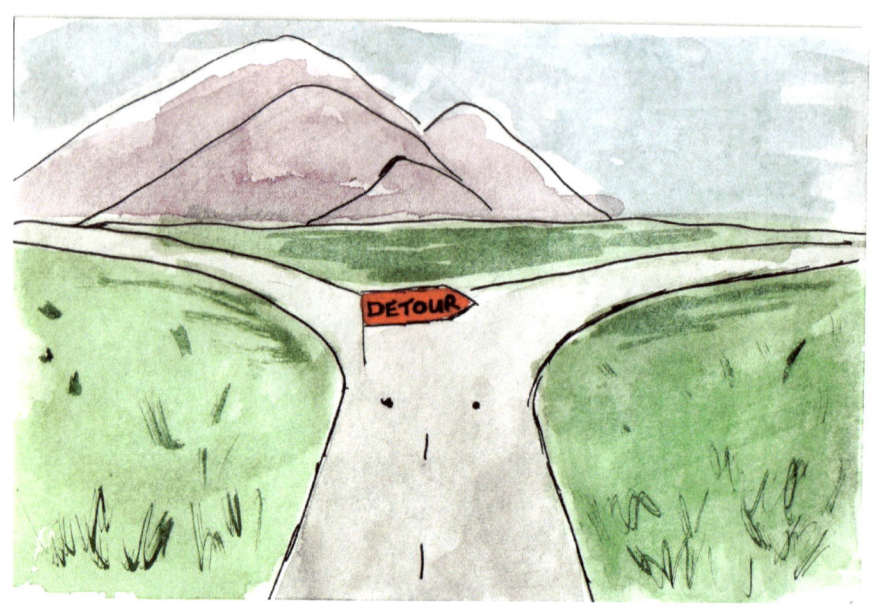

6: Detour

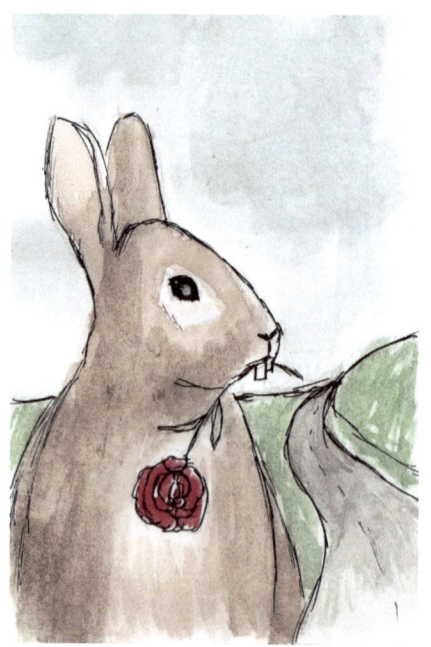

7: Alliteration

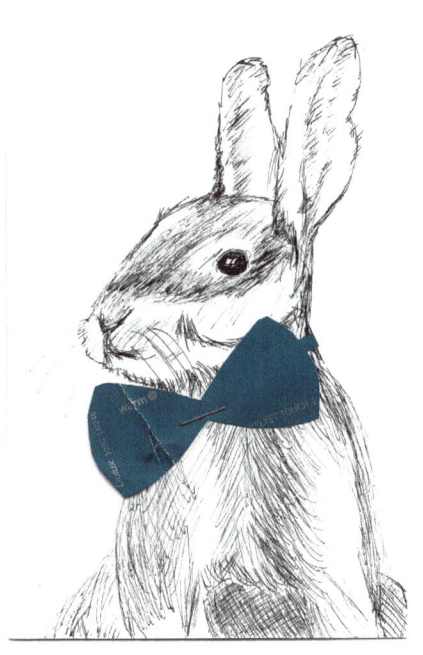 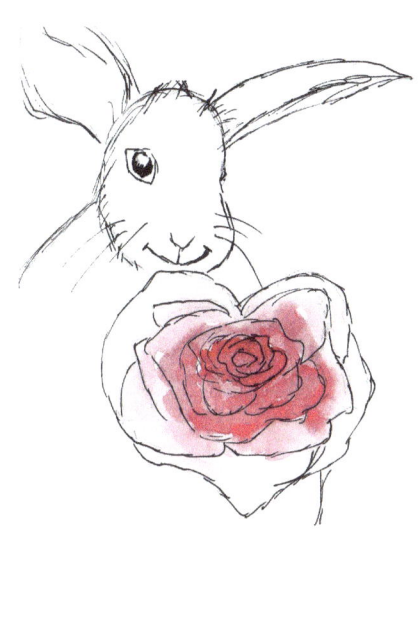

8: Paint chips   9: Ombre

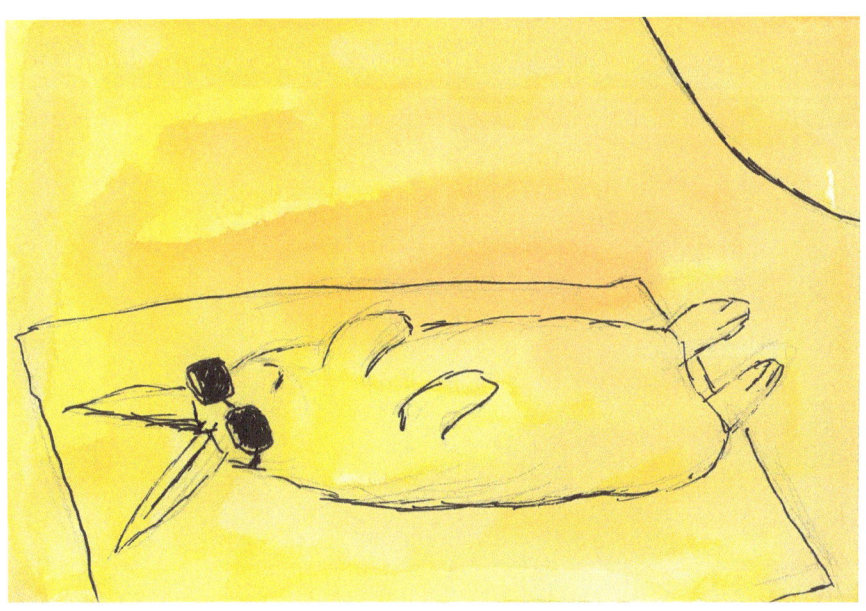

10: Sunshine yellow

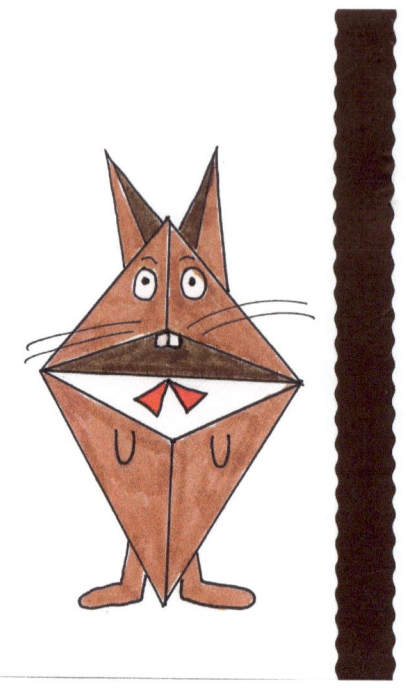

11: Tetrahedron

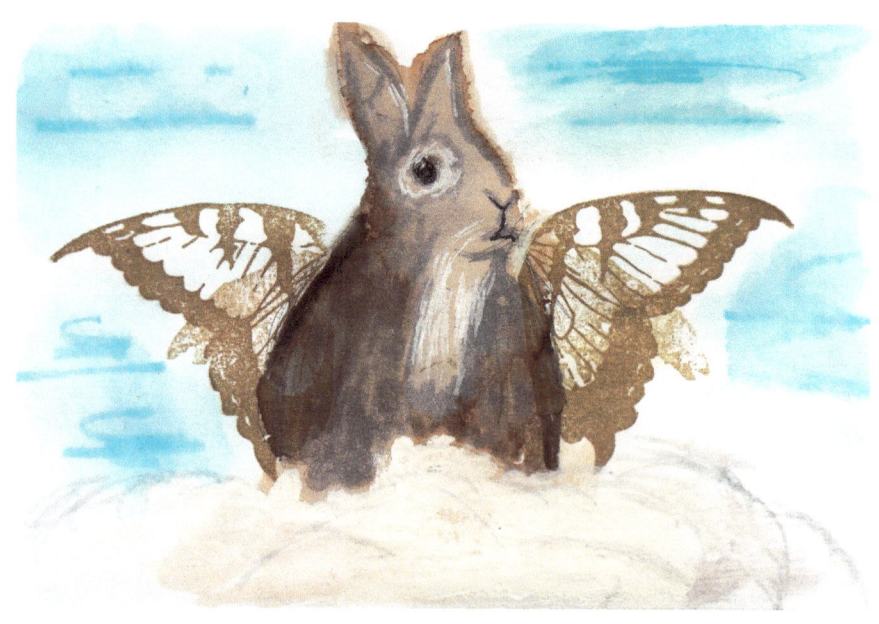

12: Wings

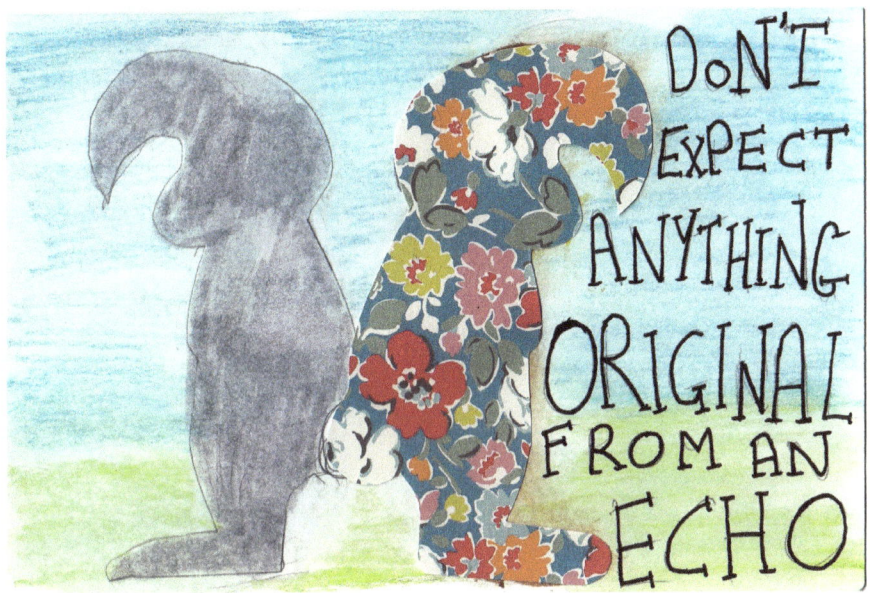

13: Echo

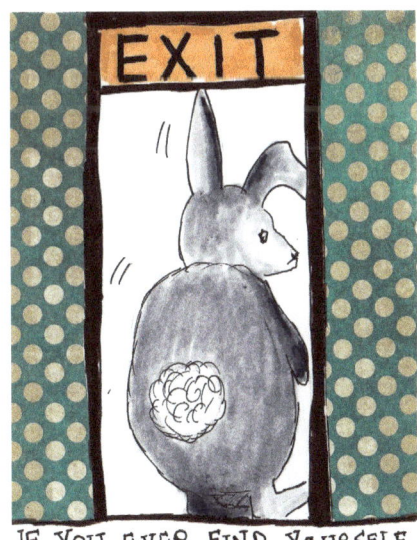

14: Leaves

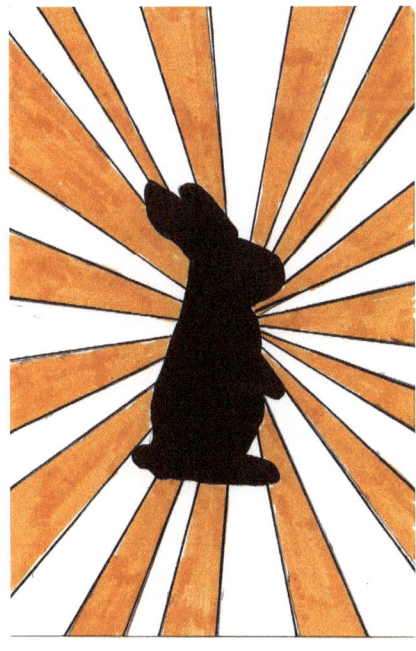

15: Starburst

16: Rainbow

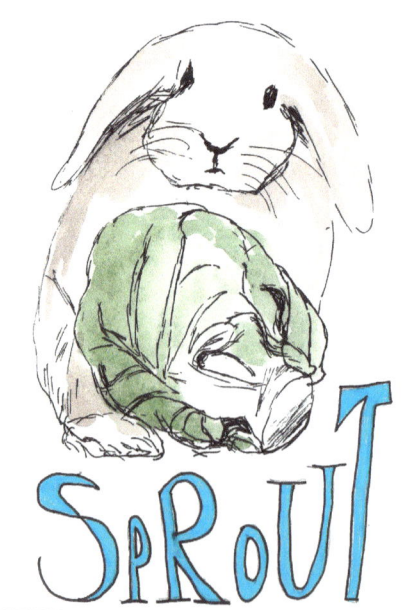

17: Sprout

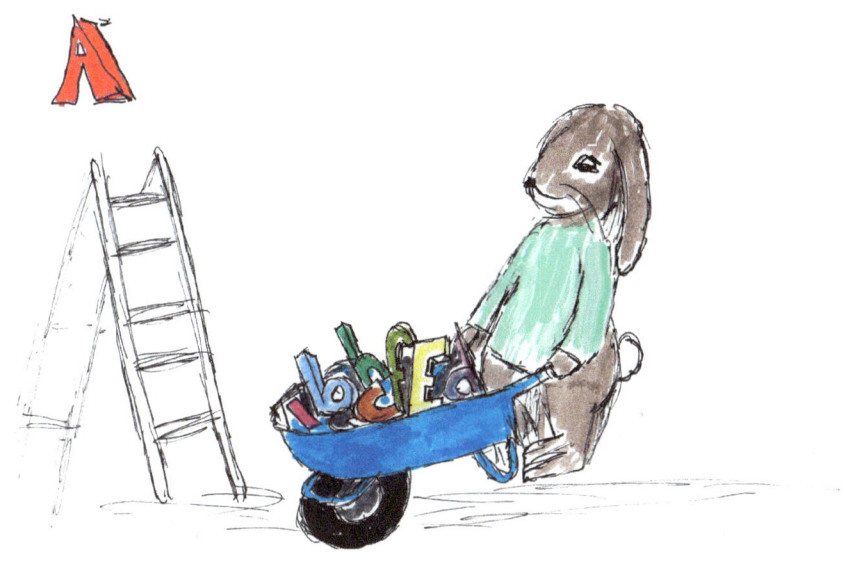

18: Alphabetise

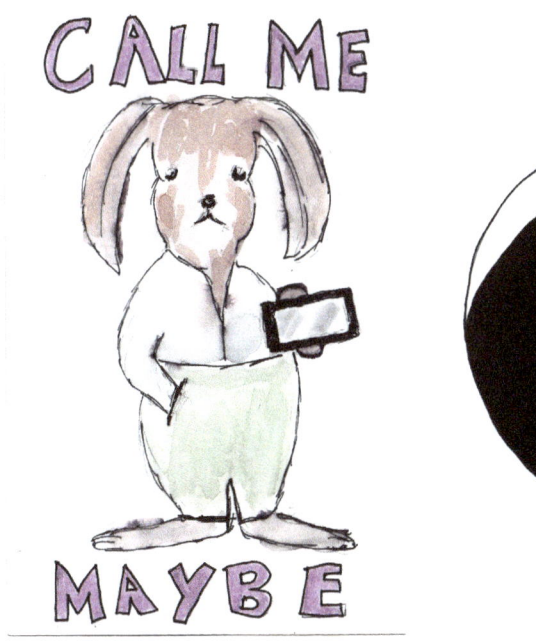

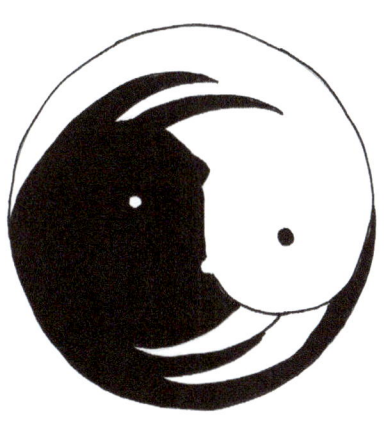

19: Gadget

20: Yin/Yang

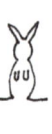
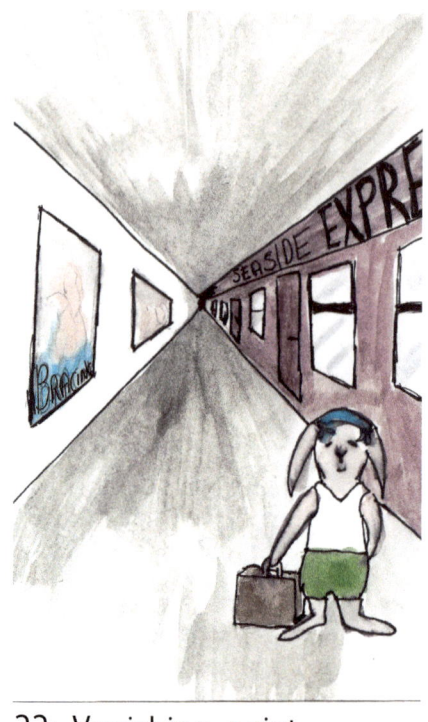

21: Simplicity22: Vanishing point

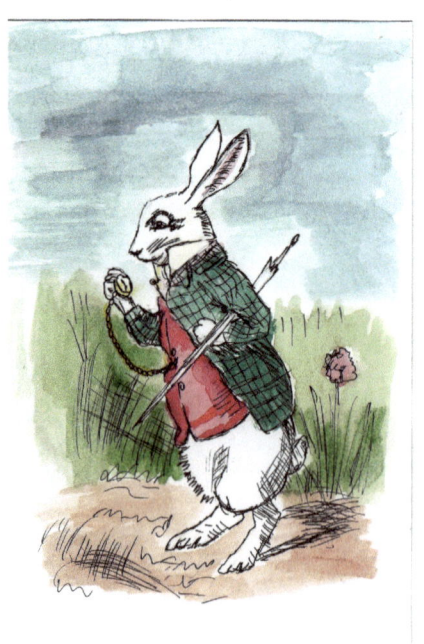

23: Alice in Wonderland

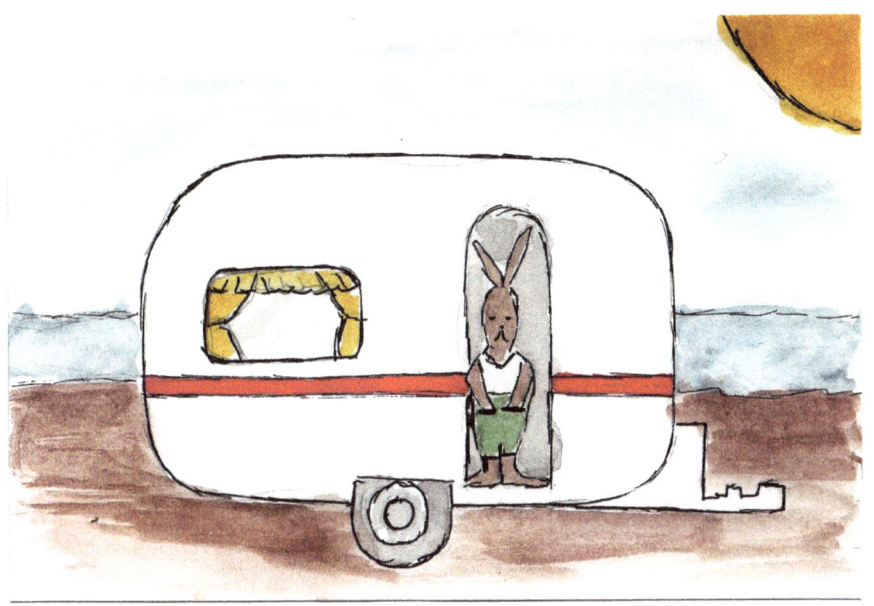

24: Caravan

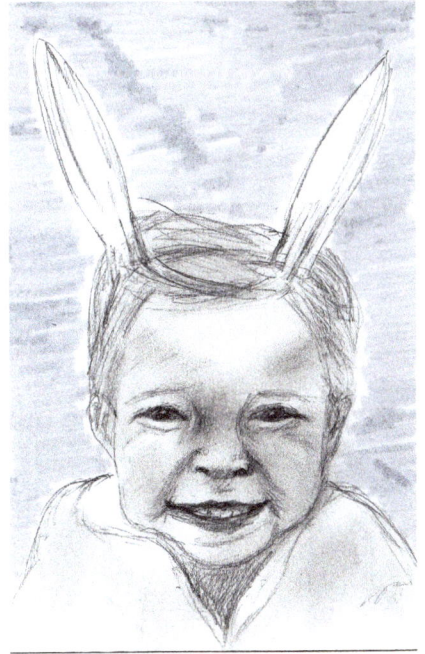

25: Portrait

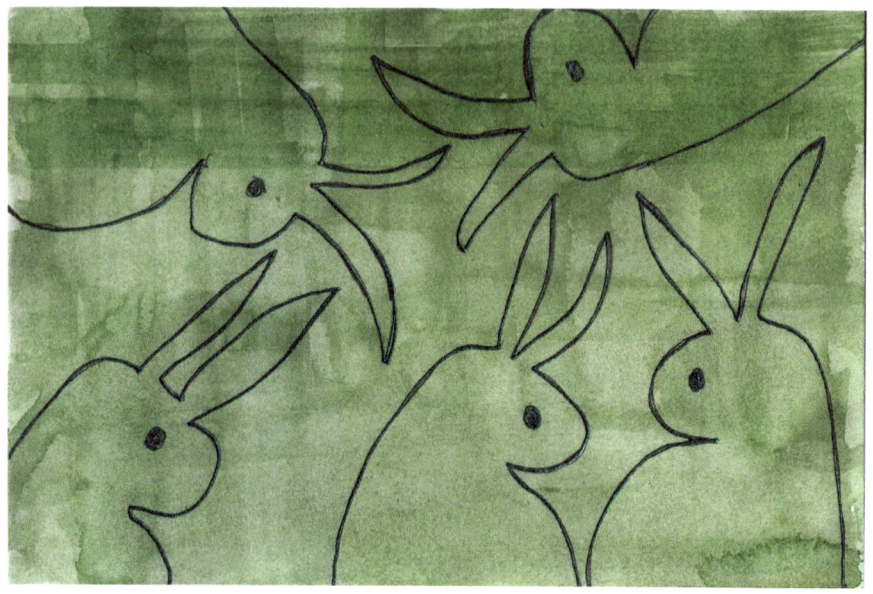

26: Green

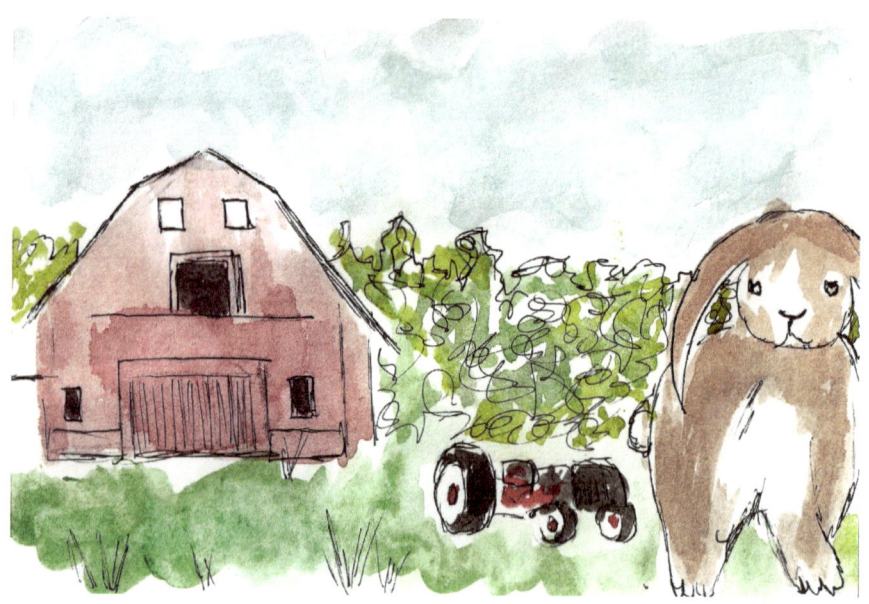

27: Farm

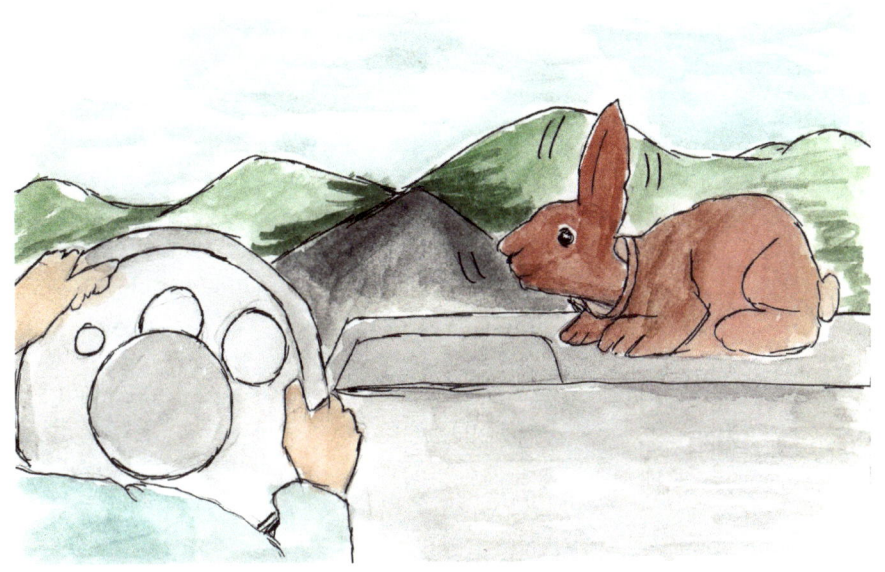

28: Dashboard

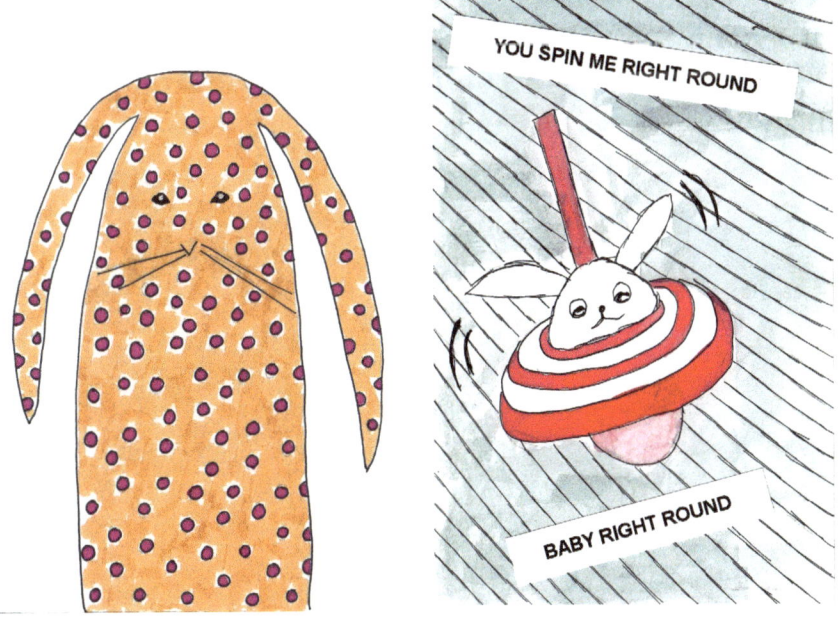

29: Polka dots

30: Gyroscope

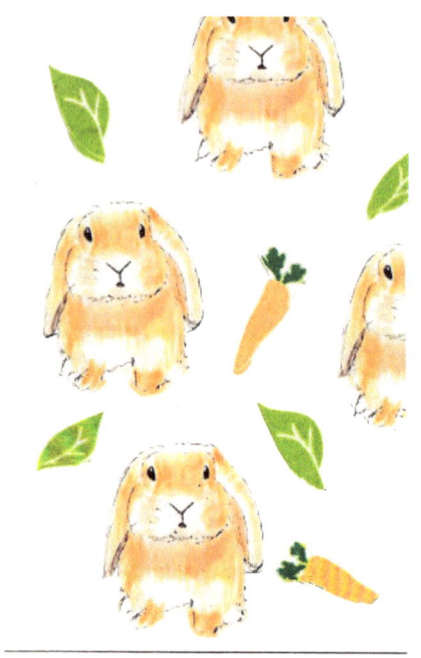

31: Faux wallpaper

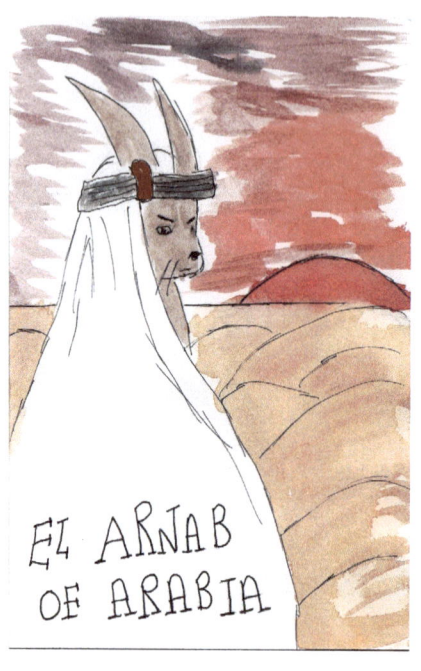

32: Desert

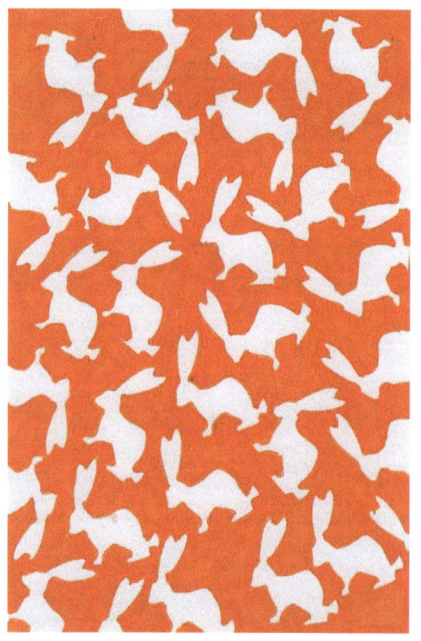

33: Orange

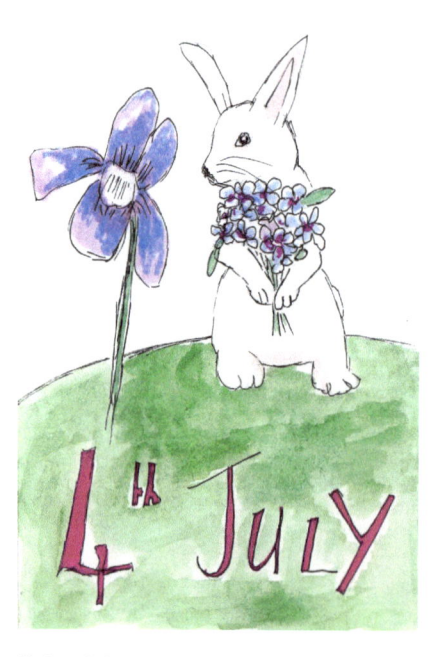

34: 4th July

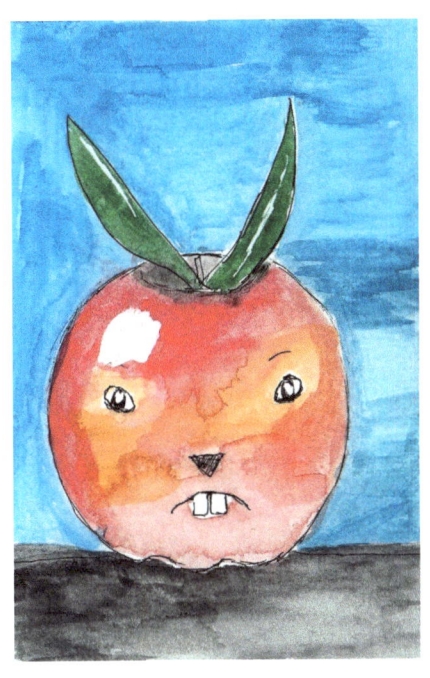
35: Apple

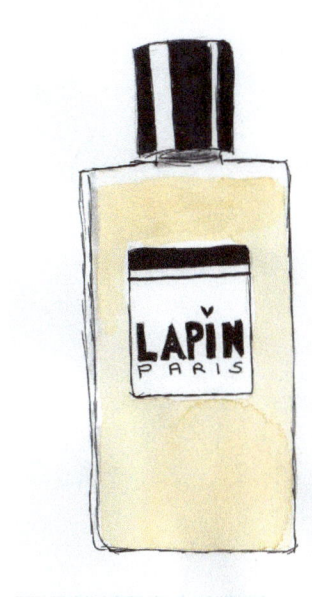
36: Perfume

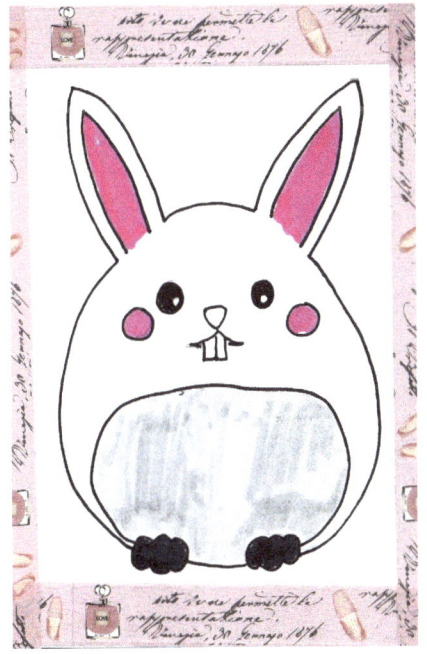
37: Kaomoji or emoji

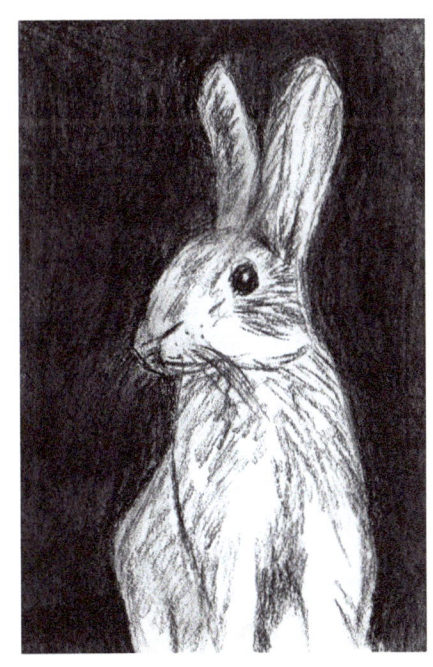
38: Charcoal

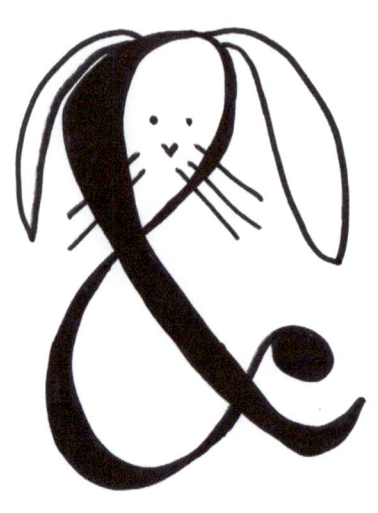

39: Ampersand

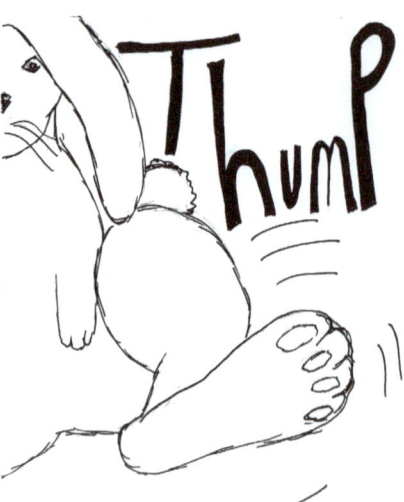

40: Steampunk

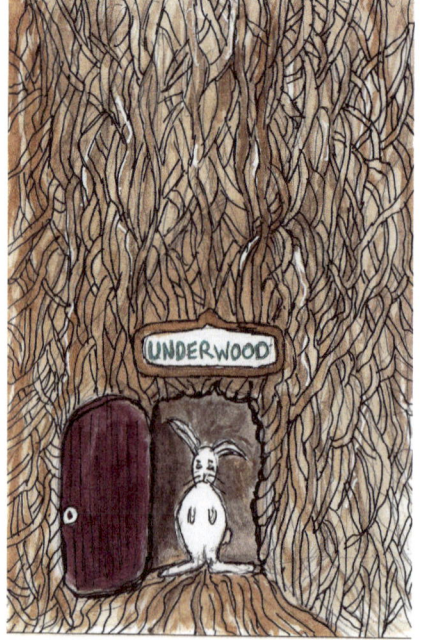

41: Roots

42: Onomatopoeia

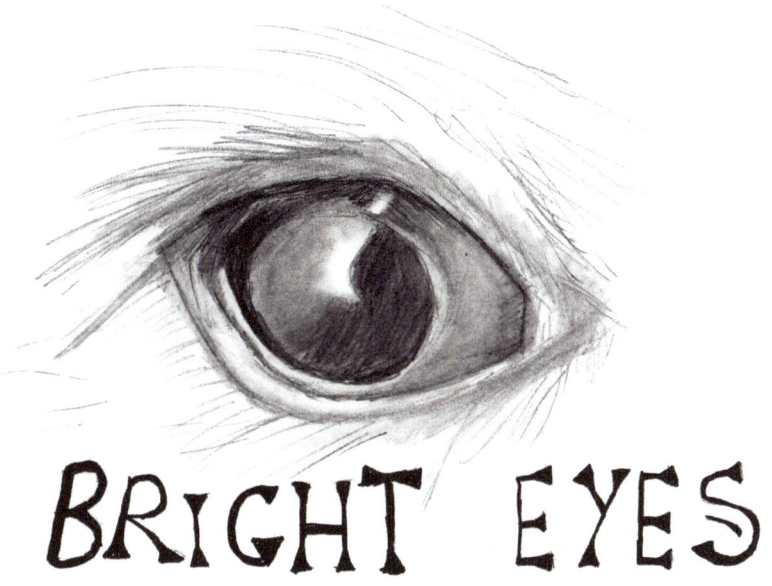

BRIGHT EYES

43: Lyrics

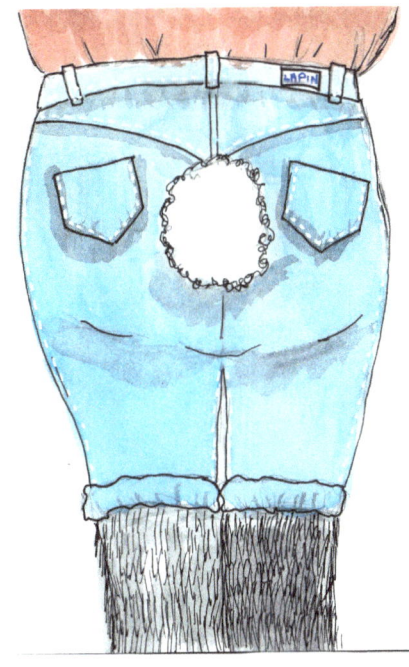

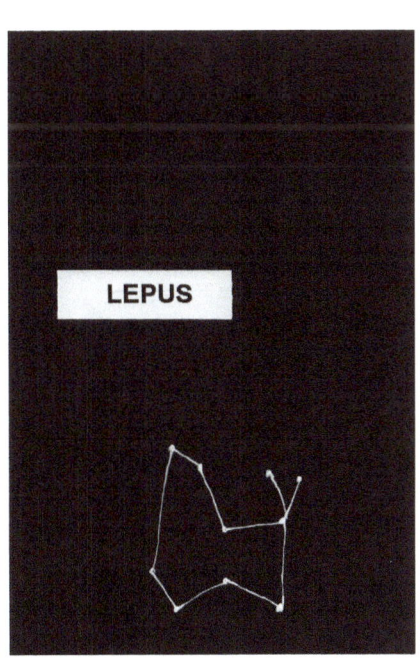

44: Denim

45: Night sky

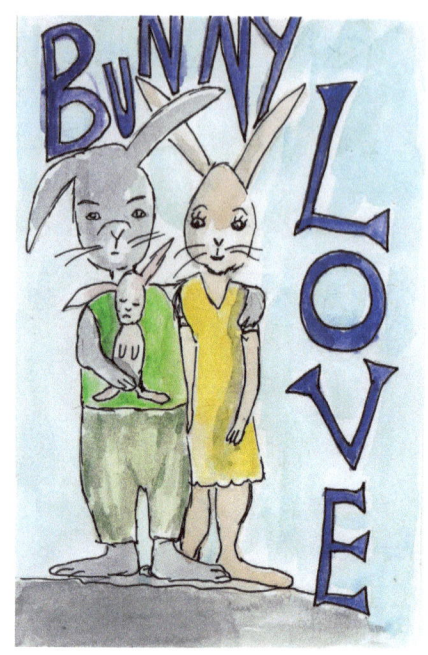

46: Love

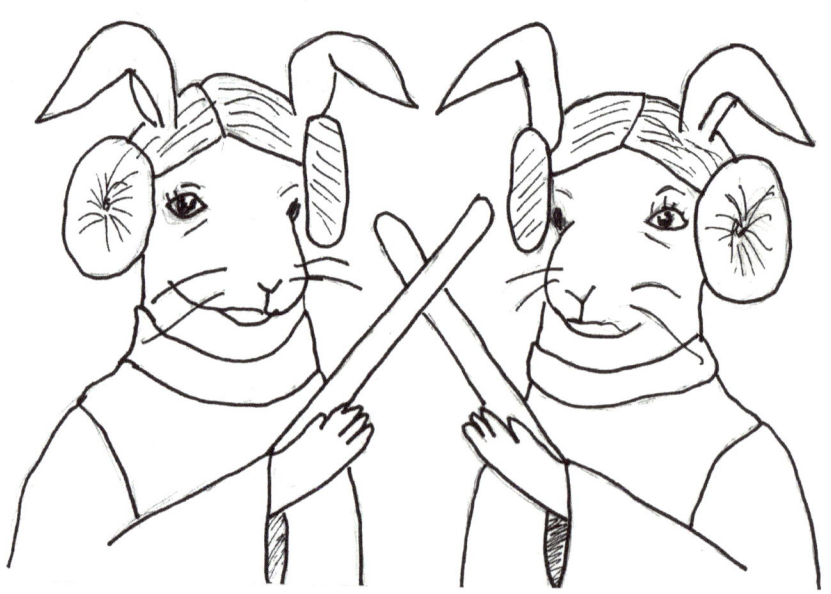

47: Layers

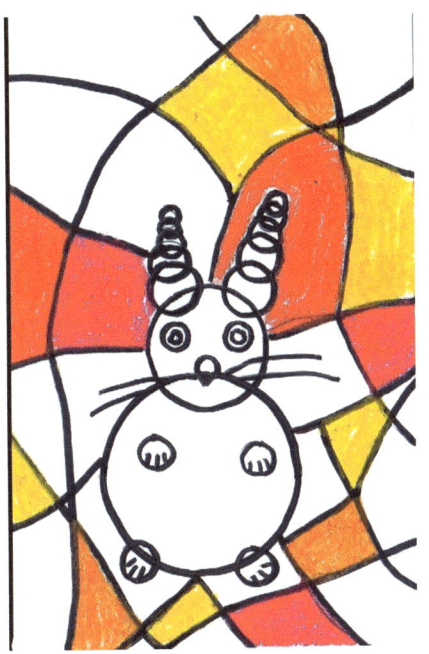

48: Intersection

49: Charm bracelet

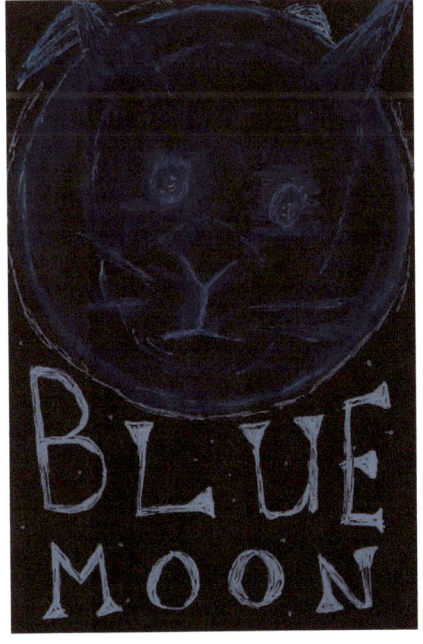

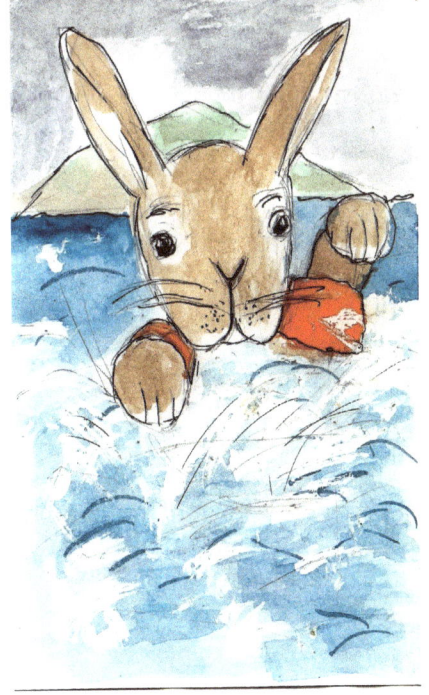

50: Sun or moon

51: Swim

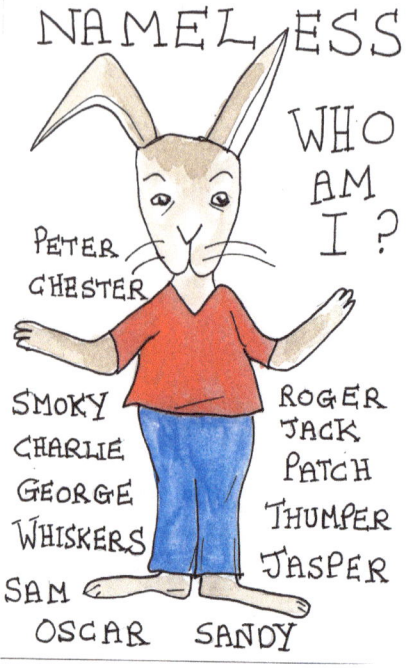

52: Adjective

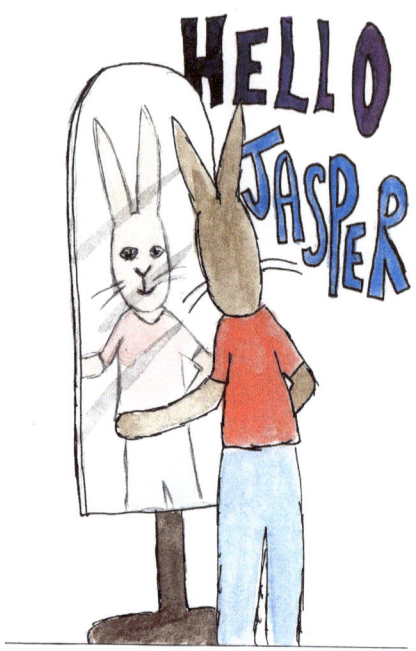

53: Mirror

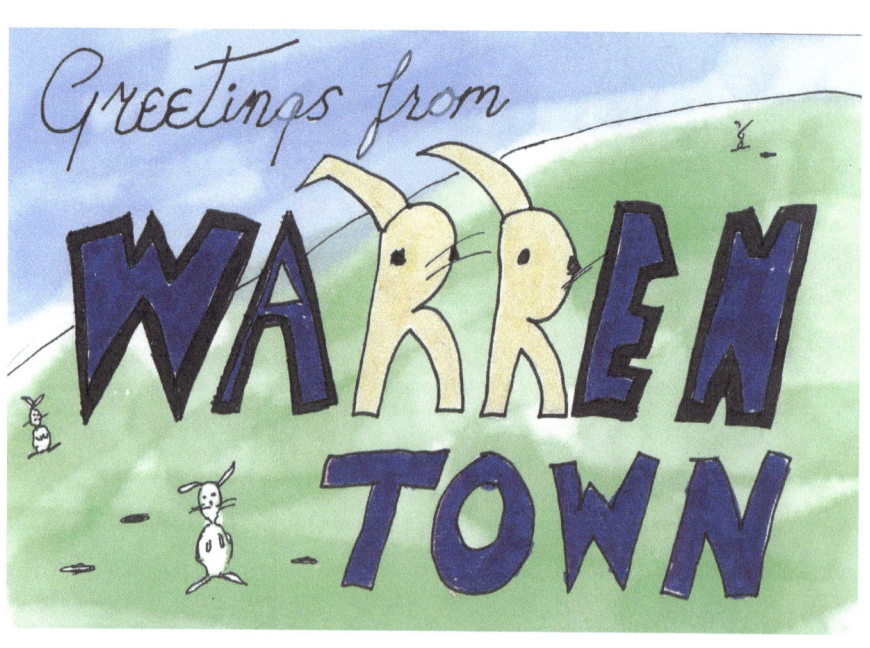

54: Greetings from....

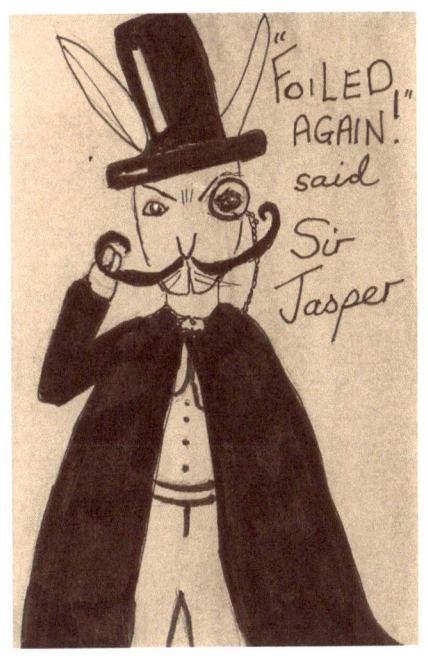

55: Sepia

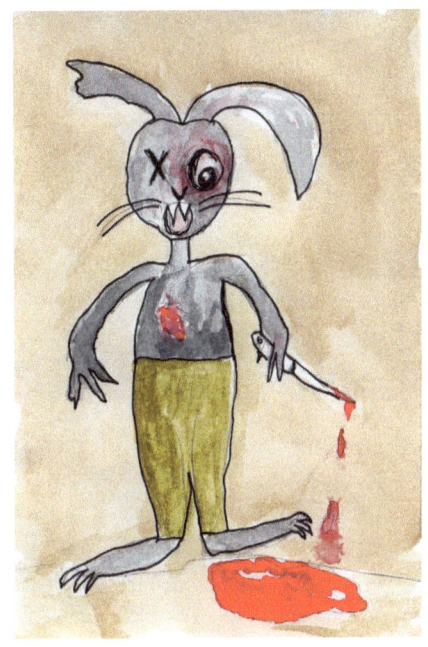

56: Zombie

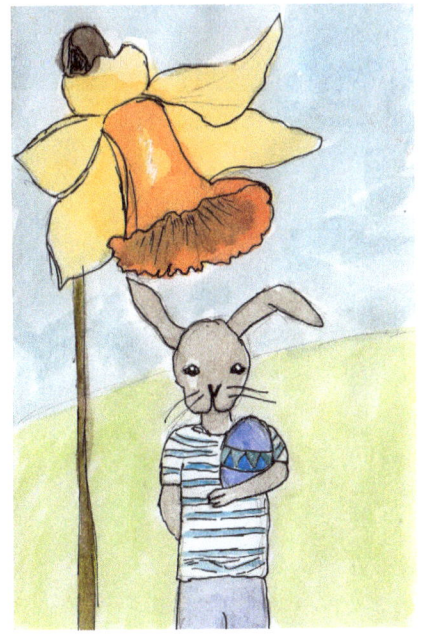

57: Spring

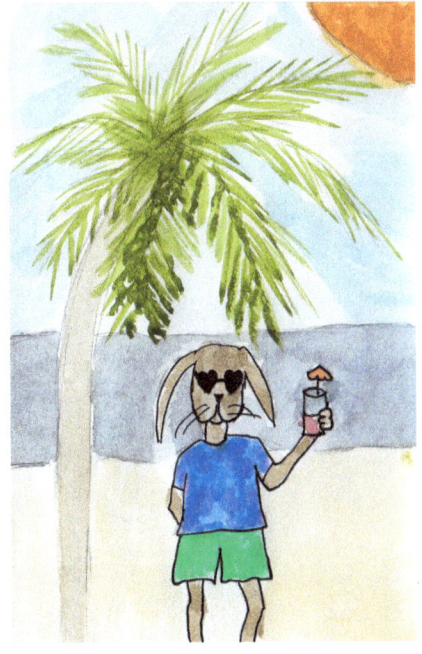

58: Summer

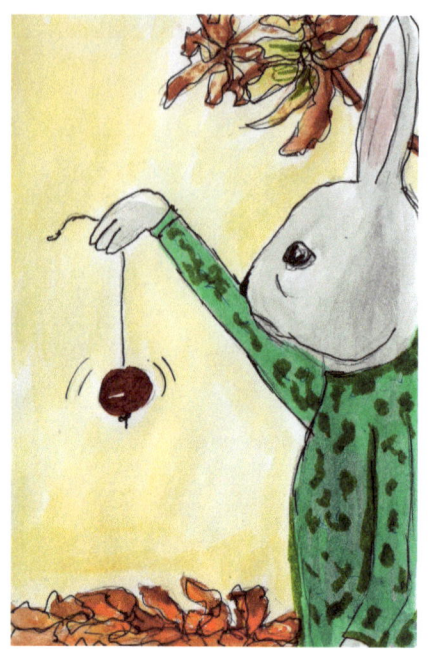
59: Autumn

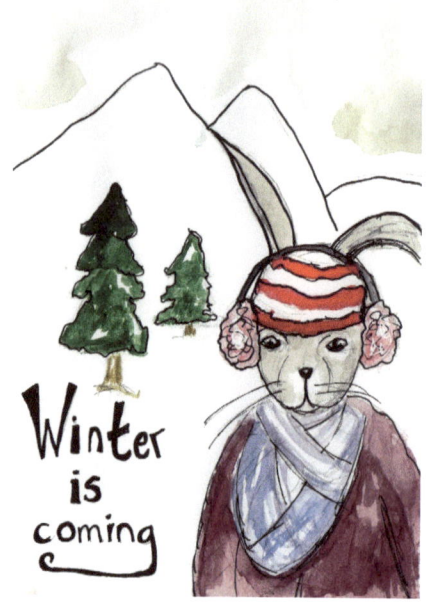
60: Winter

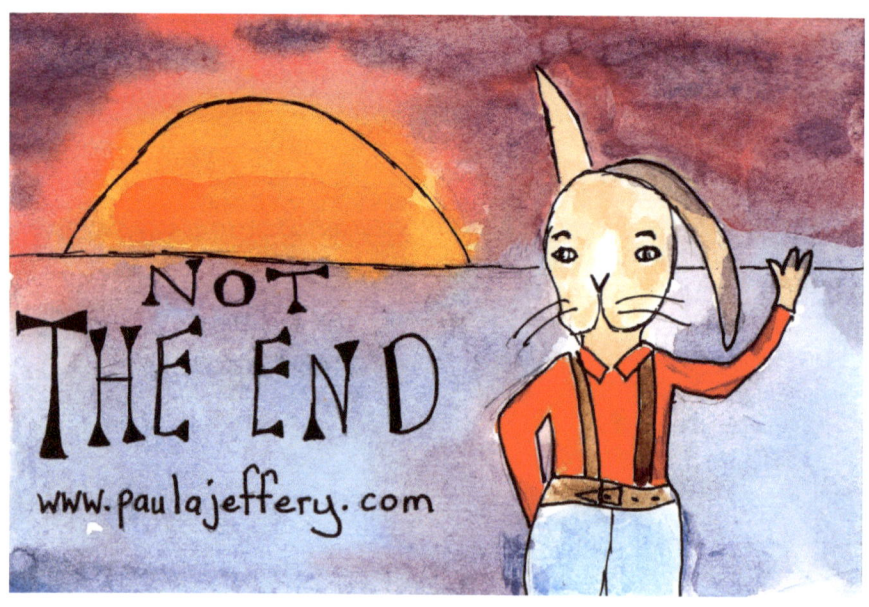
61: Sunset

Other books by Paula Jeffery

Chasing Rainbows
 a genealogical journey

Dog Days
 The Art of the Dog

Available from amazon.com
and amazon.co.uk

Website: paulajeffery.com
Facebook: facebook.com/paula.jeffery1
Instagram/Twitter pjscribble

www.ingramcontent.com/pod-product-compliance
Lightning Source LLC
Chambersburg PA
CBHW040303220526

45473CB00002B/573